# 105

# HALLOWEEN

# JOKES FOR

# KIDS

## THE SPOOKILY FUNNY

## HALLOWEEN GIFT BOOK

## FOR BOYS AND GIRLS

Association and a Committee of Publishers and Associations.

In no way is it legal to reproduce, duplicate, or transmit any part of this document by either electronic means or in printed format. Recording of this publication is strictly prohibited and any storage of this document is not allowed unless with written permission from the publisher.

The information provided herein is stated to be truthful and consistent, in that any liability, in terms of inattention or otherwise, by any usage or abuse of any policies, processes, or directions

## Q: WHO WON THE SKELETON BEAUTY CONTEST?

A: Nobody

## Q: WHAT DO SKELETONS SAY BEFORE EATING?

A: Bone appetit!

## Q: WHERE DO BABY MUMMIES GO DURING THE DAY?

A: Dayscare centres

**Q: WHO DID THE ZOMBIE TAKE WITH HIM TO THE PROM?**

A: His ghoul friend

**Q: WHAT IS A MUMMY'S FAVORITE SHAKESPEARE PLAY?**

A: Romeo and Ghouliette

**Q: WHAT MEDICINE DO YOU GIVE TO A VAMPIRE WITH A COLD?**

A: Coffin Drops

## Q: WHAT'S DRACULA'S FAVORITE PET?

A: His bloodhound

## Q: WHY DID THE VAMPIRE LEAVE HIS BASEBALL TEAM?

A: Because he was only allowed to be bat boy.

## Q: WHAT DO WITCHES USE TO KEEP THEIR HAIR IN PLACE?

A: Scare spray

**Q: WHAT DO YOU GET FROM CROSSING BAMBI AND A GHOST?**

A: Bamboo

**Q: WHICH ONE OF COUNT DRACULA'S RELATIVES HAS A BILL AND WEBBED FEET?**

A: Count Duckula

**Q: WHAT DOES TWEETY SAY WHEN TRICK OR TREATING?**

A: Twick or tweet

**Q: WHERE DO GHOSTS LIKE TO SWIM?**

A: In Lake Erie

**Q: WHAT HAPPENED TO THE GUY THAT DIDN'T PAY HIS EXORCIST?**

A: He got repossessed!

**Q: WHAT DO GHOSTS EAT FOR LUNCH?**

A: Boo-logna sandwiches

**Q: WHAT IS THE RATIO OF A PUMPKIN'S CIRCUMFERENCE TO ITS DIAMETER?**

A: Pumpkin pi


**Q: WHERE DO GHOSTS GO SHOPPING FOR FOOD?**

A: At the ghost-ery store!


**Q: WHERE DO GHOSTS MAIL THEIR LETTERS?**

A: At the ghost office.!

## Q: WHAT RIDES DO GHOSTS LIKE THE MOST?

A: Roller ghosters

## Q: HOW DO YOU FIX A BROKEN JACK-O-LANTERN?

A: By using a pumpkin patch.

## Q: WHEN DOES A SKELETON LAUGH?

A: When someone tickles its funny bone.

**Q: WHY WAS THE MUMMY SO TENSE?**

A: Because he was all wound up.

**Q: WHERE DID THE GOBLIN THROW THE FOOTBALL?**

A: Over the ghoul line.

**Q: WHAT DO SKELETONS ORDER AT RESTAURANTS?**

A: Spare ribs

## Q: WHAT DO GHOSTS MAIL HOME WHEN ON VACATION?

A: Ghostcards

## Q: WHY DO WITCHES WEAR NAME TAGS?

A: So they know which witch is which.

## Q: WHAT DO YOU CALL TWO WITCHES SHARING THE SAME ROOM?

A: Broom mates

## Q: WHAT IS A WITCH'S FAVORITE SUBJECT IN SCHOOL?

A: Spell-ing

## Q: WHY DID THE WITCH STOP TELLING FORTUNES?

A: Because there was no future in it!

## Q: HOW DO YOU MAKE A WITCH ITCH?

A: Take away the "w"!

**Q: HOW IS A WITCH'S FACE LIKE A MILLION DOLLARS?**

A: Both are green and wrinkly.

**Q: WHY ARE GHOSTS SUCH TERRIBLE LIARS?**

A: Because you can see right through them!

**Q: WHAT IS DRACULA'S FAVORITE BUILDING IN NEW YORK CITY?**

A: The Vampire State Building

**Q: WHAT DO VAMPIRES FEAR THE MOST?**

A: Tooth decay

**Q: WHAT DID THE BAT SAY TO HIS GIRLFRIEND?**

A: I like to hang out with you.

**Q: WHY DIDN'T ANYONE WANT TO LOOK AFTER THE BABY VAMPIRE?**

A: Because he was a pain in the neck!

**Q: WHAT DID THE KID VAMPIRE SAY WHEN HE WENT TO BED?**

A: Turn on the dark because I'm afraid of the light.

**Q: WHAT'S A VAMPIRE'S FAVORITE FOOD?**

A: Stake

**Q: HOW DO YOU JOIN A VAMPIRE FAN CLUB?**

A: By submitting your name, address, phone number and blood type!

**Q: WHAT'S A VAMPIRE'S FAVORITE FRUIT?**

A: Nectarine

**Q: WHAT'S A VAMPIRE'S FAVORITE ANIMAL?**

A: A giraffe

**Q: WHY DON'T SKELETONS LIKE GOING TO PARTIES?**

A: Because they have nobody to take!

**Q: HOW COME THE PIRATE BOUGHT HIS EARRING AT THE DOLLAR STORE?**

A: Because it was a buck-an-ear!

**Q: WHAT IS A PIRATE ALWAYS LOOKING FOR EVEN THOUGH IT'S RIGHT BEHIND HIM?**

A: Booty

**Q: WHY DIDN'T THE SKELETON SCORE ANY GOALS?**

A: Because he had no heart.

**Q: WHICH MONSTER LIKES TO PLAY TRICKS ON HALLOWEEN?**

A: Prankenstein

**Q: WHAT GENRE OF MUSIC DO MUMMIES LIKE?**

A: Wrap music

**Q: HOW DO GHOSTS WASH THEIR HAIR?**

A: With shamboo

**Q: WHAT IS A MONSTER'S FAVORITE DESSERT?**

A: I scream

**Q: WHAT IS A SCARECROW'S FAVORITE FRUIT?**

A: Straw-berries

**Q: WHAT HAPPENS WHEN A VAMPIRE GETS LOST IN THE FOG?**

A: He is mist.

**Q: WHAT ROOM IN THE HOUSE DOES A ZOMBIE NOT NEED?**

A: The living room

**Q: WHEN IS IT BAD LUCK TO BE FOLLOWED BY A BLACK CAT?**

A: When you're a mouse!

**Q: WHAT HAPPENS IF A VAMPIRE STAYS IN THE SNOW TOO LONG?**

A: Frostbite

## Q: WHAT'S BIG AND SCARY AND HAS 3 WHEELS?

A: A monster riding a tricycle!

## Q: WHAT POSITION DO ZOMBIES PLAY IN HOCKEY?

A: Ghoulie

## Q: WHAT DO YOU CALL A WITCH THAT GOES TO THE BEACH?

A: A sandwitch

**Q: WHAT SORT OF PANTS DO GHOSTS WEAR?**

A: Boo-jeans

**Q: WHY DID THE ZOMBIE SKIP SCHOOL?**

A: Because he felt rotten inside!.

**Q: WHAT IS A VAMPIRE'S FAVORITE FOOD?**

A: Blood orange

**Q: WHAT DID THE KIDS SAY WHEN THEY HAD TO CHOOSE BETWEEN THEIR TRICYCLES AND CANDIES?**

A: Trike or treat

**Q: WHAT INSTRUMENT DOES A SKELETON PLAY?**

A: The trombone

**Q: WHAT DID THE CAT SAY TO HER BOYFRIEND ON HALLOWEEN?**

A: You're purr-fect for me!

**Q: WHAT CANDY DO YOU EAT ON THE PLAYGROUND?**

A: Recess pieces

**Q: WHAT IS A GHOST'S NOSE FULL OF?**

A: Boooogers

**Q: WHAT DO BIRDS LIKE TO SAY ON HALLOWEEN?**

A: Trick or tweet

**Q: WHAT DO GHOSTS LIKE TO PUT IN THEIR PANCAKES?**

A: Boonanas and Booberries

**Q: WHAT ROADS DO GHOSTS LIKE TO HAUNT?**

A: Dead ends

**Q: WHO DID THE GHOUL INVITE TO HIS BIRTHDAY PARTY?**

A: Anyone he could dig up!

**Q: WHAT KIND OF COOKIES DO MONSTERS PREFER?**

A: Ghoul scout cookies

**Q: WHAT DID THE SKELETON SAY WHEN HE WAS RIDING HIS HARLEY?**

A: I'm bone to be wild

**Q: WHY DO VAMPIRES THINK THEY ARE GOOD ARTISTS?**

A: Because they like to draw blood!

**Q: WHEN DO GHOULS LIKE TO COOK THEIR VICTIMS?**

A: On Fry Day

**Q: WHAT KIND OF CANDY DO VAMPIRES ENJOY THE MOST?**

A: Suckers

**Q: WHAT DO YOU CALL A MONSTER WITH A BROKEN LEG?**

A: Hoblin Goblin

**Q: WHAT DO ZOMBIES LIKE TO DRINK ON A HOT SUMMER DAY?**

A: Ghoul-aid

**Q: WHEN DOES A GHOUL HAVE BREAKFAST?**

A: In the moaning!

**Q: WHAT DO GHOSTS LIKE WITH THEIR COFFEE?**

A: Scream and sugar

## Q: WHAT DO GHOSTS LIKE TO EAT FOR DINNER?

A: Spookghetti

## Q: WHAT'S A GHOST'S FAVORITE FRUIT?

A: Booberries

## Q: WHERE DO VAMPIRES USUALLY EAT LUNCH?

A: At the casketeria.

**Q: WHY WAS THE GHOUL SUCH A MESSY EATER?**

A: Because he was always goblin!

**Q: WHAT DO MONSTERS LIKE ON THEIR SUNDAES?**

A: Whipped scream

**Q: WHAT SONG DOES DRACULA HATE THE MOST?**

A: You Are My Sunshine

**Q: WHAT MONSTER LOVES DANCE MUSIC?**

A: The Boogieman

**Q: WHY DO GHOSTS LIKE GOING OUT SO MUCH?**

A: Because they love to boo-gie!

**Q: WHAT DO GHOSTS SAY WHEN THEY THINK SOMETHING IS NEAT?**

A: "Wow, that's ghoul!"

**Q: WHY WAS THE GHOST ARRESTED FOR SCARING YOUNGSTERS?**

A: Because he didn't have a haunting license!

**Q: WHERE DID THE GHOST THROW THE FOOTBALL?**

A: Over the ghoul line!

**Q: WHAT DO YOU CALL A GOBLIN WHO GETS TOO CLOSE TO THE FIRE?**

A: A toasty ghosty

## Q: WHAT KIND OF MAKEUP DO GHOSTS WEAR?

A: Mas-scare-a

## Q: WHO IS THE MOST FAMOUS GHOST DETECTIVE TO EVER LIVE?

A: Sherlock Moans

## Q: WHERE DO MOST OF THE WEREWOLVES LIVE?

A: Howllywood, California

**Q: WHERE DO MOST GOBLINS LIVE?**

A: North and South Scarolina


**Q: WHAT DO YOU CALL A LITTLE MONSTER'S PARENTS?**

A: Mummy and Deady


**Q: HOW CAN YOU TELL A VAMPIRE HAS BEEN IN A BAKERY?**

A: All the jelly has been sucked out of the jelly doughnuts.

**Q: HOW DO VAMPIRES FLIRT?**

A: They bat their eyes!

**Q: WHY DOESN'T ANYONE LIKE DRACULA?**

A: Because he has a bat temper!

**Q: WHO DOES DRACULA GET LETTERS FROM**

A: From his fang club!

**Q: WHY DID THE VAMPIRE NEED COLD MEDICINE?**

A: In order to stop coffin!

**Q: WHAT CAN'T YOU GIVE THE HEADLESS HORSEMAN?**

A: A headache

**Q: WHY DID THE HEADLESS HORSEMAN GO START A BUSINESS?**

A: He wanted to get a-head in life!

**Q: WHERE DO GHOSTS LIKE TO GO ON VACATION?**

A: Mali-boo

**Q: WHERE CAN YOU FIND A WITCH'S GARAGE?**

A: In the broom closet!

**Q: WHY DO WITCHES RIDE BROOMS?**

A: Because the vacuum cleaner's power chord is too short!

## Q: WHY DON'T ANGRY WITCHES RIDE THEIR BROOMS?

A: They're afraid of flying off the handle!

## Q: WHAT HAPPENED WHEN TWO VAMPIRES WENT OUT ON A BLIND DATE?

A: It was love at first bite!

## Q: WHY DID THE GHOST GO INTO THE BAR?

A: To get some boos!

**Q: HOW COME DRACULA NEVER GOT MARRIED?**

A: He never met the right ghoul!

**Q: WHO DID DRACULA TAKE TO THE MOVIES?**

A: His ghoul-friend

**Q: WHAT DO OWLS SAY WHEN THEY GO TRICK OR TREATING?**

A: Happy Owl-ween!

**Q: WHERE DO GHOSTS USE THEIR BOATS?**

A: The Eerie Canal

**Q: WHO ARE A WEREWOLF'S COUSINS?**

A: What-wolf, who-wolf, when-wolf and how-wolf!

**Q: WHERE DO WEREWOLVES STORE THEIR BELONGINGS?**

A: In a were-house

**Q: WHAT DO WEREWOLVES READ TO THEIR CHILDREN BEFORE SLEEPING?**

A: Hairy tails

**Q: WHAT DO ITALIAN GHOSTS EAT FOR DINNER?**

A: Spookghetti

**Q: WHAT GROWS IN THE GARDENS ON HALLOWEEN?**

A: Zombeets

**Q: WHAT KIND OF TREAT IS NEVER ON TIME?**

A: ChocoLATE

**Q: WHICH ONE OF THE WITCH'S FRIENDS WAS GOOD AT BASEBALL?**

A: The bat!

**Q: WHAT GHOST LIVES IN TOWN HALL**

A: The night mayor

**Q: WHAT DO THE MONSTERS USE TO CLEAN THE ICE AFTER HOCKEY GAMES?**

A: A Zombieoni

**Q: WHAT WAS THE MUMMY MUSICIAN'S FAVORITE NOTE?**

A: The dead sea

**Q: WHY DID THE TRAVELLING WITCH THROW UP?**

A: She was broomsick!

**Q: WHERE DO GHOSTS LIKE TO WATER SKI?**

A: Lake Erie



**Q: WHAT KIND OF MISTAKES DO SPIRITS MAKE?**

A: Boo boos



**Q: WHAT TYPE OF TREES DO GHOSTS LOVE?**

A: Ceme-trees

## Q: HOW CAN MONSTERS TELL THEIR FUTURES?

A: By reading their horrorscopes!

## Q: WHAT AMUSEMENT PARK RIDE DO GHOSTS LIKE THE MOST?

A: Roller ghosters

## Q: HOW DO GHOSTS LIKE THEIR COFFEE?

A: 2 sugars and 2 screams!

**Q: WHY CAN'T YOU SEE A GHOST'S MOTHER AND FATHER?**

A: Because they're transparents!

**Q: WHY DON'T PEOPLE LIKE VAMPIRES?**

A: They have bat tempers!

**Q: WHAT KIND OF MUSIC DO GHOSTS LISTEN TO?**

A: Spiritual music

## Q: WHY DIDN'T THE SKELETON CROSS THE ROAD?

A: He didn't have the guts!

## Q: WHAT HAPPENED TO THE WITCH WITH THE UPSIDE DOWN NOSE?

A: Her hat blew off every time she sneezed!

## Q: WHAT DO MONKEY GHOSTS LIKE TO EAT?

A: Boonanas

**Q: WHAT SPORT DO VAMPIRES LIKE THE MOST?**

A: Batminton

**Q: WHY CAN'T SKELETON MUSICIANS PERFORM AT CHURCH?**

A: Because they have no organs!

**Q: WHAT DOES IT TAKE TO BECOME A VAMPIRE?**

A: Deadication

## Q: WHY DID THE ZOMBIE QUIT HIS TEACHING JOB?

A: Because he only had 1 pupil left!

## Q: WHO DO COWBOY ZOMBIES FIGHT?

A: The Deadskins

## Q: WHAT DOES A ZOMBIE GET WHEN HE'S LATE FOR A DATE?

A: The cold shoulder

**Q: HOW ARE ZOMBIES LIKE COMPUTERS?**

A: They both have megabites!

**Q: WHERE DO ZOMBIES GO ON VACATION?**

A: To the Deaditerranean!

**Q: WHO WON THE ZOMBIE RACE?**

A: Nobody. It was DEAD even!

**Q: WHAT'S A BABY ZOMBIE'S FAVORITE TOY?**

A: A deady bear

**Q: WHAT CANDY DO GHOULS HATE THE MOST?**

A: Life Savers

**Q: WHAT KIND OF VEHICLE DO ZOMBIES DRIVE?**

A: Monster trucks

**Q: WHAT DID THE ZOMBIE SAY AFTER EATING THE COMEDIAN?**

A: This tastes funny!

**Q: WHY DID THE ZOMBIE JOIN THE ARMY?**

A: He heard they gave out arms!

**Q: WHY DIDN'T THE ZOMBIE GET THE ROLE IN THE MOVIE?**

A: The director wanted someone more lively!

**Q: WHAT'S BLACK, WHITE AND DEAD ALL OVER?**

A: A zombie penguin

**Q: WHY DID THE ZOMBIE COMEDIAN GET BOOED OFF STAGE?**

A: Because all his jokes were rotten!

**Q: WHY DID THE ZOMBIE GO NUTS?**

A: He lost his mind!

Knock Knock!

Who's there?

Ice Cream.

Ice cream who?

Ice cream every time I see a ghost!

Knock, Knock!!

Who's there?

Olive.

Olive who?

Olive Halloween!

Knock, Knock!!

Who's there?

Howl!

Howl who?

Howl you be dressing up this Halloween?

Knock, Knock!!

Who's there?

Frank.

Frank who?

Frankenstein!

Knock Knock!!

Who's there?

Boo.

Boo Who?

Ah, don't cry, Halloween is just around the corner!



Knock, Knock!!

Who's there?

Ivan.

Ivan who?

Ivan to suck your blood!!

Knock, Knock!!

Who's there?

Phillip.

Phillip who?

Phillip my bag with Halloween candy!




Knock, Knock!!

Who's there?

Jacklyn.

Jacklyn who?

Jacklyn Hyde!

Knock, Knock!!

Who's there?

Essen!

Essen who?

Essen it fun to listen to these Halloween jokes!

Knock, Knock!!

Who's there?

Iran!

Iran who?

Iran over here to get some candy!

Knock, Knock!!

Who's there?

Voodoo!

Voodoo who?

Voodoo you think you are!

# THANK YOU FOR READING AND HAPPY HALLOWEEN!

CPSIA information can be obtained
at www.ICGtesting.com
Printed in the USA
LVHW012219230820
663969LV00019B/2773